Parts Of Me
Lost And Found

Cisel Ozbay

ISBN: 979-8654502872

DEDICATION

To all those who have helped me find myself.

CONTENTS

LOST AND FOUND

ACKNOWLEDGMENTS

Many thanks to all my friends and family who have supported my writing, and to those who have given me inspiration.
A special thanks to my sister Sultan Ozbay who has helped with the illustration of the cover.

FIND

To be yourself, you need to find yourself.

And that is all life really is -

Finding yourself.

INSANITY

The most profound truths are found at the border of insanity.

In the moment where you know absolutely nothing for sure

When you have let go of all your preconceptions and biases

Yet when you have access to infinite possibilities

You might then find the freedom to discover your truth.

ASH

Anger has fired up

Burnt me down

Into ashes.

I rise -

Almost a stranger to myself

I know exactly where things used to be

But I have no proof of their existence within me.

CONTRAST

Contrast is important, it provides context.

Without contrast it is difficult to find meaning, for there is no point of reference.

No understanding of the other, the opposite, the whole.

TIME

Isn't it unfortunate that the more we figure out what we want in life, the less time we have to find it?

FRICTION

Anxiety is like friction.

The more you think, the more it builds up.

The solution is in the simple art of letting go.

FEAR

Don't be afraid to accept fear.

In fact, fully immerse yourself in it.

For if you fail to face your fear, you will be bound to perpetual anxiety.

SILENCE

Silence can be uncomfortable for someone suffering from anxiety.

It can be scary because you are burdened

With the sound of your own thoughts

And there is nothing distracting you from them.

It is a beautiful thing when you begin to find peace in silence.

SLEEP

You can use sleep as a form of escapism

As a way to take a break from the noise of your own conscious mind.

But isn't it unnerving – the moments where you half wake up and all the thoughts come rushing back?

Which nightmare do you prefer?

PEACE

Pain is only unmanageable if you cannot make sense of it.

Once you begin to compartmentalise and register an experience

There is no longer a need to fear it.

It is fear of the unknown that causes anxiety

With knowledge and acceptance you will find peace.

CLARITY

Understanding is dependent on one's ability to attain a state of calm.

If you try to look down at your reflection

in a lake disturbed by waves

It will be impossible to see yourself clearly.

And if you try to analyse a situation

Or make sense if yourself when you are overwhelmed with emotion

You will find yourself in a similar predicament.

Clarity -

In all its forms, is unable to accommodate disturbance.

CHAOS

Be the stillness you seek in the chaos you find yourself-

For chaos exists not to a calm mind.

MIND

Concern does not equate to responsibility.

A peaceful mind is a sign of maturity.

STILL

Sit in silence-

And listen wholeheartedly to the thing you've been trying to distract
yourself from.

VOICES

There are so many voices in your head -

Sometimes it becomes difficult to know which one is you.

That is why it is so essential to quieten your mind -

To hear yourself again.

CONCIOUSNESS

True consciousness is not knowledge

But actually the absence of all thought.

For awareness of the whole

And connection to all

Requires attachment to nothing.

Like water that flows with the ocean

Is the ocean

Because it has surrendered itself wholly to it.

BARE

You see we are born bare

But life dresses up

With its expectations

And its façades.

Most of us need to go back

To being comfortable with bareness.

To dress down, instead of trying to dress up

The embrace the essence of who we are

Rather than who others want us to be.

Yes, we are born bare,

But it takes courage to walk out naked.

To let others see you

Really see you.

Not many people are able to do that.

SEEKING

And our biggest flaw was to seek happiness as something outside of
ourselves.

In things external to us.

And in a manner inconsistent with the essence of being.

By this I mean constantly looking for more,

Without realising that we were intrinsically complete,

And that all that we were seeking, already resided within us
the whole time.

INTUITION

There is comfort in knowing what to expect.

That is why those who are well connected to their intuition tend to be good at remaining calm.

ART

It is easy to capture internal peace for a moment, but it is an art to be able to make it one's nature.

FREEDOM

Freedom begins and ends in the mind.

You are free so long as you can protect yourself from the confines of what is tangible.

MEDITATION

If you master the art of meditation, nothing becomes boring.

For if you immerse yourself fully in any activity

You can transcend time in its practical sense.

You can let your mind wonder elsewhere -

Anywhere.

RAIN

There are two types of people.

Those who try to escape the rain

And those who enjoy getting soaked in it.

The latter have grasped the method of being content in life.

FLAWS

There is a fine line between self- criticism and self- doubt.

Be aware of your flaws -

But never underestimate your ability to overcome them.

MOTION

Man is nothing without purpose,

And indeed he defines himself through the progress he makes.

Move in the direction of your desire,

That is the least you can do to feel alive.

EFFORT

There is nothing worse than living a stagnant life.

For all effort is rewarded; it either works out for you, or you learn a lesson from it.

In either case, you've lost nothing.

FEEL

Love deep

Feel intensely

So that when it is time to walk away,

There is nothing else you could have done.

ALL

And my problem was not being able to give a little

It was all or nothing

Raw and honest.

Too intense for the ordinary person

Used to truths diluted

And conversations softened

By those who would rather be civil than real.

I could fake it I'm pretty sure

Be disingenuous I mean

But I don't think I have the energy

Or the heart for it.

Sincere is what I am

Sincere is what I crave

Sincere is what I will wait for.

LESSON

You can lose a person but you cannot lose a lesson.

Be grateful for the experience of them.

CLOSURE

Closure has nothing to do with the other person hearing your goodbye.

It depends entirely on how sincerely you mean it.

GENUINE

Time weighs little against the importance of a lesson or the depth of
a connection.

Genuine moments of revelation, or those of mutual understanding,
Mean a lot more than a superficial forever.

If only we could all learn
To appreciate this.

FORGIVENESS

Forgiveness heals.

Maybe it is too late for the relationship -

But it is never too late to heal your own heart.

LAUGH

Laugh from the bottom of your heart

Don't be afraid to allow yourself to feel joy fully.

I know you've been hurt

But wasn't it worth it?

GROWTH

It is not time which makes a man grow

Rather the depth of his experiences.

DEPTH

It is a good thing to feel more deeply than others, it makes you grow
faster.

But sometimes it becomes a burden

To carry your emotions

And to make it seem like you don't have any.

MISTAKES

Too much balance can be toxic too.

We must make mistakes as human beings, and we must not be afraid of doing so.

We must not stop growing - that is the worst thing we can do for ourselves.

FUTILE

I see it

You see it

Who will tell him

That his efforts are futile?

Or maybe the effort is the thing

Is the lesson.

You don't really see it

Neither do I.

But he eventually will.

PHILOSOPHY

Question your own philosophy before you reject another.

For we are far more likely to be slaves of our own current state of mind

And far less likely to learn nothing from the other.

STUDY

Study the self as you would any other person you want to know well.

With the same depth and scepticism.

You will reveal to yourself just as much, if not more.

WISE

Being wise means not knowing more than the average man

But being deeply aware of the limits of what you do and don't know.

STORIES

It is amusing

To hear the stories

That people can make up about you

And even more amusing

To observe them

Without getting offended.

RARE

We all seek to be understood.

To be reassured that we are not alone in the way we think.

Isn't it unfortunate that the rarest minds will end up feeling the loneliest?

FACE VALUE

People show you what you mean to them.

Don't look too deep

Don't deliberate on possibilities

Take it at face value.

ALIVE

You see when you are in pain

You are alive

To every inch of your being.

It is becoming numb that we should be afraid of

Of feeling nothing at all.

HUMAN

Pain reminds a man that he is human - in fact, there is nothing more real than pain.

But taken too far, it has the effect of itself desensitising him, losing its meaning as a catalyst for growth.

HEAVY

Sometimes it all becomes too heavy.

I want to scream until my lungs are depleted.

Until it feels like I have emptied the weight off my chest.

So that I can breathe again.

Lightly.

Without being suffocated by all that I have to carry

By the burden of silence.

Will you take me somewhere

A place where my voice will become drowned.

I am going to scream

It's the only thing I need right now.

If I don't let it go,

It will consume me.

SLAM

People mistake your open-heartedness for weakness.

Not realising that when the wind is strong enough, the widest doors slam shut the hardest.

REVENGE

There is no better revenge than withdrawing your energy from
someone who craves a response.

CRY

Cry - sometimes you're letting go of things you didn't even know you
were holding on to.

HEAL

If you don't stop to heal yourself

The next thing that starts well

Will end in the same way

Because of the same problem.

Don't waste opportunities by refusing to learn lessons.

INTENTIONS

Have pure intentions.

It matters in the end only for your own sanity.

RIGHTEOUSNESS

We have no control over lies

Of when the truth will come out.

So live in your truth

You shall be blessed with the comfort of authenticity.

And when the truth reveals itself

Soon or later, you shall be on the side of righteousness.

SEED

Be like the seed in the fruit:

Let the fruit ripen around you

But be unwavering in your core

And in your own truth.

Make sure that the substance of the seed remains the same

So that the essence of your being

Can be eternal.

LIAR

You may think you're fooling others - even get a thrill from getting away with it.

But believe me, one day your guilt will be a lot stronger than your excitement.

Dishonesty is destructive

Mostly to the self.

DECEIT

Humans are equipped to deal with most pain

But deceit is not of this kind.

We can't seem to comprehend this

we are deeply disturbed by lies.

Firstly because deceit, by its nature

is not something you can foresee or prepare yourself for.

And secondly, because it involves accepting the fact that you have
been inferior to the deceiving force and that you have misplaced your
trust.

This destroys the ego and one's sense of pride.

SPEAK

When you can, speak without hurting the other

But where this is not possible, do not fear being too frank or undiplomatic

So long as your honesty and integrity cannot be questioned.

PROMISES

Promises are made by those who either want to break their word, or fear doing it.

Those who really intend to execute won't need to make promises

Their actions will be proof of their intentions.

STAY

People come and go.

Sometimes because they want to.

Sometimes because they can't help it.

In any case, depending on someone staying is probably the most stupid thing you can do.

CHOICE

If you want someone to choose you

Freely and willingly,

Do not hold on to them too tightly.

For the most immediate instinct of anyone who feels hostage,

Is escape -

It is to break free completely.

AUTHENTIC

The fear of being different and its connotations of alienation is the enemy of authenticity.

TRUTH

Objective truth exists not

For we are all subjective beings

And the perspective of one person is not superior to another

The truth - is simply what we make of it.

SIMPLE

Simple is boring only to the superficial observer.

WORDS

Sometimes words lose their meaning the more of them you try to use.

COMPROMISE

I don't compromise myself for anyone anymore.

For some reason, this makes many people uncomfortable -

People like to think they have control over you.

NOBLE

A noble man -

Is a man that is acutely aware of his intrinsic value without letting this feed his ego.

INSECURITY

True confidence is silent.

It is only insecurity which creates the need for a man to strive in order to overcompensate for his weakness.

YOU

If you focus on your relationship with others

And source your validation from this,

You will end up merely weak and discombobulated.

If instead, you expend your efforts building a sound relationship with
who you are

No experience can rattle you

Nor your sense of identity.

SHINE

Oh young girl

Don't hold on to things so tightly.

Let it go and it shall find you.

It is futile trying to catch light

Let it shine on you.

WOMAN

There is something mesmerising in the stance of a woman who knows herself.

Who knows her worth and her boundaries.

A woman who can love unconditionally

But above all, a woman who can love herself first.

WHO?

If they ask me: who are you?

I can't guarantee that the answer I give today will do for tomorrow.

In fact, I sincerely I hope it does not.

I AM

I am both the sea

And the drop of water that splashes offshore.

I am both the sun

And the ray of light that glistens onto the flower.

I am both the apple

And the seed that ripens within it.

I am both the mother

And the child.

I am the whole

And I am the part.

For one exists not without the other.

The part is the whole

As the whole is the part.

I am both.

ABOUT THE AUTHOR

Cisel Ozbay is an author from London who began writing during her time at university in Aberdeen. She was inspired by her own life experiences and the turbulent times in her life. Her Parts Of Me: From Me to You, and Parts Of Me: Lost and Found books contain poems written during this same period in her life.

LOST AND FOUND